THE DAVID SERIES #1

A Story of Faith and Courage from Young David

Retold by
Dr. Veronika Amaku

Illustrated by
Jadyn Richardson

RAISING FOUNDATIONS OF MANY GENERATIONS

Copyright © 2023 by Veronika Amaku

Published in 2023 by Ambassador Publishing. All rights reserved. No part of this book may be used or reproduced in any manner whatsoever without written permission except in the case of brief quotations embodied in critical articles and reviews

Scripture quotations are taken from the Holy Bible, New Living Translation, copyright ©1996, 2004, 2015 by Tyndale House Foundation. Used by permission of Tyndale House Publishers, Carol Stream, Illinois 60188. All rights reserved.

Art Direction and Book Design by Toluwanimi Babarinde

Illustrations by Jadyn Richardson

Send inquiries to ambassador.publish@gmail.com

Hardcover ISBN: 978-0-9788390-1-7

Paperback ISBN: 978-0-9788390-2-4

Audio Book ISBN: 978-0-9788390-0-0

Published in the United States of America

For Young Readers

My goal is to inspire young readers through relatable, captivating stories highlighting David's courage, perseverance, failures, and faith.

He would often sing and play fine tunes for the sheep on his harp, and he cared for them like they were his friends.

He also saw to it that they were well-fed and safe. Of course, the sheep knew his voice, and they followed him wherever he went.

David, acknowledging God as the source of his victory, bowed down in worship and thanked God for providing him with the strength, courage, and knowledge to protect the sheep from the lion.

David's confidence in God and what he did show us how to handle problems and temptations that the enemy brings into our lives.

The following are lessons we can learn from David's encounter with the lion:

Jesus is our shepherd. Like David, Jesus cares about us. He provides for our daily needs and protects us from danger.

But just as the sheep followed David, we must listen to him. Can you imagine what would happen to the sheep if they did not stay with or listen to David?

The first step is for us to accept Jesus into our lives.

Pray: God, I admit that I am a sinner, and I believe that Jesus paid the penalty for my sins by dying on the cross. I confess my sins and accept Jesus into my heart. Amen.

There is an enemy who is going around looking for someone to destroy. Therefore, we must be vigilant and prepared.

Just as David was attentive to the signs of danger around him, we must be aware of the presence of the enemy around us.

Jesus said, "The enemy, comes to steal, kill, and destroy." –John 10:10.

Sometimes, he comes through negative thoughts, immoral advice from friends, bad shows on television, movies, social media, etc.

By staying alert, vigilant, and feeding our minds with positive things from God's word, we can be better prepared to face any challenge or temptation that comes our way.

David had a good attitude.

He loved God, loved his family, listened to his dad's and great-grandma's advice, did not complain about his brothers' meanness toward him, and even loved his animals!

God wants us to have good attitudes because we will reflect His nature to those around us.

Apostle Paul wrote in 1Timothy 3:16 and 17 (NLT), "All Scripture is inspired by God and is useful to teach us what is true and to make us realize what is wrong in our lives.

It corrects us when we are wrong and teaches us to do what is right. God uses it to prepare and equip his people to do every good work."

Maintain self-control in the face of hardship.

In the face of peril, David stayed calm and composed, allowing him to think clearly and act decisively.

According to science, the area of our brain that is responsible for logic and judgment becomes impaired when we are afraid.

As a result, it is difficult to make good decisions or think clearly. Self-control is vital for making sound judgments and avoiding being paralyzed by fear or terror.

RESIST THE ENEMY. David's confidence in God enabled him to face the lion boldly.

The book of James encourages us to "Submit yourselves, then, to God. Resist the devil, and he will flee from you." James 4:7.

We must oppose the enemy by keeping firm in our faith in the face of adversity.

The story of David's experience with the lion inspired the people in his little town of Bethlehem. Share your story to encourage others.

When we share our stories of endurance, faith and God's faithfulness, we can encourage others to trust God and face their challenges with courage and conviction.

About the author

Dr. Veronika Amaku

Dr. Veronika Amaku, a devoted wife, mother, and college professor, inspires through unwavering faith.

Born again in 1983, she actively served in campus Christian organizations and as a trained worker with Children Evangelism Ministry. She nurtured young minds with the wisdom of the Bible by teaching Sunday schools and establishing Bible Clubs for children in Nigeria and the United States.

Guided by God's grace, she raised five children who love the Lord. Her life exemplifies faith's transformative power. Her children's books impart values of love, faith, and compassion, touching young hearts worldwide.

She is a remarkable author and role model.

About the series

The David Series is a collection of children's books that feature the biblical David as the protagonist.

The goal is to inspire young readers through relatable, captivating stories highlighting David's courage, perseverance, failures, and faith.

To keep children engaged, we incorporated an art style that is highly adept at evoking emotions and bridging the gap between classic and modern tales.

Furthermore, the illustrations' inclusive nature promote diversity and expose youngsters to different artistic styles and cultures, cultivating a deep appreciation for the arts.

Heartfelt Appreciation

Words can barely describe my immense gratitude toward everyone who has been a part of this remarkable journey. Bringing this book from thought to life has been a group effort filled with passion, creativity, and tireless dedication.

I give the glory to God for the inspiration and guidance toward making this book a reality. I pray that this book brings faith and life to readers across the globe.

Dr. Toluwanimi Babarinde, you have been the backbone of this project, and your contributions have been invaluable.

Jadyn Richardson, you are a gem. You breathed life into our characters with your anime-style artistry. You captured the story's essence and added a unique charm that will surely captivate our young readers.

Dr. Innocent Ononiwu, you paid meticulous attention to detail as a reviewer, and, despite your busy schedule, you spent hours refining each page. Thank you for your dedication to excellence.

Lastly, thanks to my husband, Dr. Samuel Amaku, whose belief in my potential has been a great source of encouragement, and to my children, Josh, Ruth, Grace, Esther, and Mary, whose confidence in this project has been a constant source of strength for me. My siblings, their families, and friends, I am grateful for your endless support, encouragement, prayers, and inspiration.

Together, we have created something that will continue to raise the foundations of many generations for eternity, even after we go Home. This book is not merely a product of ink and paper but a God-inspired expression of our collective creativity, passion, and determination.

With heartfelt thanks,
Dr. Veronika Amaku
Ambassador Publishing

www.ingramcontent.com/pod-product-compliance
Lightning Source LLC
Chambersburg PA
CBHW042141290426
44110CB00002B/83